His Faith Works

His Faith Works

By: Robert King

Published By:
Good News Fellowship Ministries

Copyright Information

His Faith Works
By: Robert King

All scripture quotations are from:
The New King James Version
(NKJ)

Published and Copyright © 2017 by
Good News Fellowship Ministries
220 Sleepy Creek Rd.
Macon, GA 31210

ISBN-13: 978-1-888081-37-4
ISBN-10: 1-888081-37-6

No part of this book may be reproduced or transmitted in any form or by any means, electronic or mechanical, including photocopying, recording, or by an information storage and retrieval system, without permission in writing from the Author.

Cover Designed and Formatting Lisa Walters Buck

Contents

CHAPTER 1
Not Enough Faith   1

CHAPTER 2
Unity In The Faith   13

CHAPTER 3
The Sovereignty Of God   21

CHAPTER 4
How Faith Comes   33

CHAPTER 5
Faith Made Manifest   45

CHAPTER 6
The Gift of Faith   55

Chapter 1
NOT ENOUGH FAITH

This false teaching of 'not enough faith' has been rampant in too many pulpits for far too long. So many times I have witnessed, especially among healing ministries, this cruel and damaging teaching. I've seen and heard firsthand, ministers ask the sick person in their prayer line before praying for their healing, *"Do you have faith for this?"* I've witnessed these same people marching an individual who's in great pain up and down the front of the church trying to get them healed, requesting they lift their painful leg and try kicking it to see if they've been healed. When the individual then explains that actually their condition remains exactly the same, the cruel and false teaching is often repeated: *"Oh, you don't have enough faith."* I recall seeing this during my years of Pastoring. Visiting ministers would pray for sick members of the church but not only was nobody healed, but sadly a great increase of pain and worsening of their conditions was common place. Again, they always had their 'trump-card' to fall back on when the person they were praying for wasn't healed. 'They didn't have enough faith!'

Didn't even Jesus tell Peter off for his little faith…?!

For those of you who don't know me, in 2003 the Holy Ghost visited me. I never recovered. Before this I would go into the pulpit completely prepared. Every word was written down. By the time I had read from the beginning to the end of my notes that would give me my twenty five minute sermon. That was the way I functioned. One of the things which happened in that initial encounter is that He took me away from preparing messages and having full sermon notes. This was a rather difficult time for me as all I knew was to have full notes. When you are used to this and suddenly you find yourself stood up without any notes, it is an uncomfortable position to be in. God was taking me to something new and something different and I struggled with letting go of my comfort blanket. Over a period of just a few weeks I had gone from full sermon notes to no notes at all. I literally stood in front of the people and opened my mouth and let God fill it. And fill it He did. All those years before hand I had spent fifteen hours studying to be able to write six pages and suddenly all that went out of the window. Since this time of Holy Ghost habitation I no longer prepare sermons nor messages but rather I prepare me. That way when I stand up I can hear the voice of God. I open wide my mouth so He can fill it and that way the people get a 'now word.' They don't get a historical word because I have been tucked into a commentary, but rather, they get a relevant message because I have been preparing myself to hear heaven.

All of a sudden the Lord spoke to me. Late one Saturday night the Lord gave me a revelation on *faith* which totally blew me away! I've shared this with other people and it has had the same liberating effects on them also. Now I am sharing this with you and I know it is going to set you free and bring you into a whole new arena of understanding faith. That night I got into bed late. I was going to be preaching in about eight hours time. Suddenly, the Lord spoke to me and said,

> *"You know in the Word where I said to Peter, 'Oh you of little faith?'"*

The church think that I was condemning Peter for having little faith. But I wasn't. I was just identifying what Peter had. Peter had 'a little faith' and there was nothing wrong with that. Having a little faith was a very good thing. A little faith is what was needed and a little faith is all that was needed for Peter right now. With a little faith, Peter could actually walk on the water.

So, the Lord began to download this whole thing to me. I'm lying in bed absolutely blown away by this and thinking to myself how every sermon I have ever heard about this Scripture and every commentary I've ever read has always portrayed Jesus as telling Peter off for only having a little faith. Yet, here I am in bed hearing the Lord say that what Peter had was a good thing and that it was enough. Here was Peter actually walking on the water with a little faith Peter was walking in the supernatural realm. So Jesus wasn't telling Peter off for having a little faith. Jesus was simply identifying what Peter had: a little faith. That same little faith caused him to be able to step out of the security of the boat and walk on water. Hallelujah! By the way, you'll see many artists portray Peter up to his neck in water. But the Bible says that Peter **began** to sink. I don`t think the water went much over Peters feet before he cried out. Imagine if that was you, suddenly walking on water. How far under the water would you have to have sunk before you would have called out? Not too far I'm sure. The Lord told me that the only reason Peter began to sink was because Peter looked back at the natural realm and that act brought doubt to his supernatural walk.

So there I am lying in bed getting all this revelation. God is just too big, I don`t know whether you have ever noticed that, but God is **big**. As I received this download I said to God,

"Lord, I will preach this, you know I will. I will do whatever you tell me to do,

> *but Lord would you mind giving me some Scriptures here to back all this up."*

I knew I was going to be preaching in just a few hours time and some people might want to question me and others even take issue with me, so I wanted Scriptures ready to be able to give them. The Lord began to give me some Scriptures and one which He gave me was Matthew 17:20:

> *"If you have faith the size of a mustard seed you can say to this mountain be cast into the sea and it will be done."*

So there it was again. A little faith is enough to get the job done. A little faith is enough to walk in the supernatural.

The Lord went on to share how when somebody gives their life to Him, He immediately gives them a measure of faith. Romans 12:3. The reason He gives us this measure of faith upon conversion is so that we can please Him. The Bible says that without faith it is impossible to please God. Hebrews 11:6. God does not want anybody who has given their life to Him not to be able to please Him. So to make sure that they are able to please Him, He gives them, as a gift, a measure of ***His faith***. That measure of His faith which He gives us is enough. It's enough to be able to get the job done. If we needed more faith He would give us more faith. But the measure of faith He gives us upon giving our lives to Him is enough for us to be able to walk in the supernatural and enough to be able to hear heaven and speak in tongues and prophesy and operate in all the gifts. It's all there and it's a gift.

The Lord told me,

> *"Robert, you don't have any faith of your own."*

None whatsoever, the only faith you have is the faith which I have given to you. He told me that His faith works, that His faith is perfect faith. When we step out in His faith we cannot go wrong because His faith doesn't go wrong. You see if it was our faith, if all we had was our own faith then we could understand that there might be days when our faith has a day off and some days when it's stronger than other days. But if it's His faith then it will always work and always be powerful and always be enough to get the job done.

The next Scripture He gave me asks the question,

> *"Will I find any faith on the earth when I return?"* – Luke 18:8

Now this is a good question and one can consider that the Lord is suggesting that maybe He won't find any faith in the earth and Robert you've just said that He has given a measure of His faith to all of His people so when

He returns to the earth how can He not find faith in the earth? Well, there's a simple answer to this and it also shows something as to where the church is right now and that so much of the church isn't doing what Jesus did nor the works which He said we shall also do. Because Jesus said,

> *"All that I have been doing you too shall do and greater things still will you do." – John 14:12*

So why did Jesus ask the question,

> *"Will I find any faith on the earth when I return?"*

Here's the reason why: how many of us are actually walking in the perfect faith of Jesus, if we are being honest? The Bible says,

> *"Faith without works is dead." – James 2:17*

This is exactly what I believe Jesus was asking in this verse,

> *"Will I find any faith on the earth when I return?"*

Because Jesus will not be looking for dead faith, faith which is not being *used*; faith which is not being **walked in**. Faith only produces fruit when we walk in it, go with it and flow with it. Many Christians shy away from doing anything which the Bible tells us to do because we immediately ask the question,

> *"But what if it doesn't work?"*

This revelation will set you free from the `What Ifs` because His faith is guaranteed to work because it is **His**. His faith works, His faith is enough, His faith will and does get the job done. Hallelujah.

So I received this download on faith and went to the church the next day and shared it. It brought a great freedom and excitement to the people. People wanted the recording and some sent it to others and I heard incredible responses. The reason this had such an impact was because this wasn't something I had come up with through some commentary, but rather through a revelation from God as I lay in my bed. This is how it is meant to be, we are all meant to be hearing God. It says in the book of Revelation,

> *"The Spirit is speaking to the churches, let him who has an ear hear what the Spirit is saying." – Revelation 3:22.*

Which means He is speaking right now! One of the reasons we don't hear Him is because we don't shut up long enough to hear Him. Some years ago now, every time I would clean my teeth I would hear God. I used to share this with people. Then I had people come up to me wanting to know which toothpaste I was using! So I asked God,

> *"Lord, why is it that every time I clean my teeth I hear you?" He replied, "It's the only time you shut up long enough!"*

Now that wasn't quite the answer I was expecting, but I liked it! The Bible says to be still and know that He is God. Psalm 46:10. So it's right that we are still before Him. That way we can hear Him.

I hope this whole revelation on faith encourages you and takes you to a whole new level. Now, when we step out, we realise that we are not stepping out with just what we have of our own, but rather that we are stepping out with what He has given us: His faith. And His faith works! I want you to receive this revelation on faith, hearing it is one thing and receiving it is another. The word falls onto all kinds of different paths and soils and we don't want the weeds coming up and stealing this from you. Don't move on to the next chapter until you get this revelation. Remember, His faith never gets tired and His faith always works.

This faith is from heaven; from God Himself. We have to do something with it. We have to do something to get the faith working. Now it is very important you hear what I am about to say. Remember the occasion when Jesus went out to the disciples and walked on the water. They saw Jesus and thought that He was a ghost, but He said,

> "'It is I. Peter called out, 'Lord! If it is you, tell me to come to you on the water.' Jesus then said to Peter, 'Come.'"

Peter got out of the boat and started to walk on the water. Peter walked in the supernatural. I always think of the boat as being like the church. We are all on-board yet here we only see Peter getting out of the boat. Jesus only told Peter to, "Come." It was Peters time, his destiny, his moment. This was already preordained; already written in heaven that Peter would do this.

Side note here, we need to be careful when we see somebody's else's success, somebody else's calling, destiny, and ministry birthing right in front of us that we do not become in anyway jealous ourselves. We must never allow that old flesh to become jealous, bitter or even angry. Remember we are not meant to be walking in the flesh, but rather dying daily to it according to the Apostle Paul. 1 Corinthians 15:31. When we are in the 'boat' (church) and we see 'Peter' (another person's ministry) being launched, we should actually rejoice and celebrate with them. I just want to encourage you that when we see our brothers and sisters in Christ moving forward, that we get excited and cheer them on also, giving God the praise. As much as we might be longing for our own ministry to launch, we need to be excited for one being launched. So let's guard our hearts and not allow jealousy to creep in but keep it real and keep it Jesus.

Remember!

A little faith is enough. We don`t have any faith of our own. The only faith we have is His faith. His faith works, all of the time. His faith works because it is His.

Chapter 2

UNITY IN THE FAITH

The only faith we have is the faith which God gives to us. When we give our lives to Him, He gives us a *measure* of His faith (Romans 12:3). So outside of His faith we actually do not have any faith of our own.

The Bible speaks about *unity in the faith* (Ephesians 4:13). The reason we can have unity in the faith is because the faith is pure, the faith is holy, the faith is perfect, the faith is anointed, the faith is God's faith. His faith is all that it needs to be. It's interesting how the Bible doesn't tell us to have unity in theology and yet the Bible tells us to have unity in the faith. Why can't we have unity in other things such as theology? The answer is simple. Everyone has their own opinions, their own ideas and their own likes and dislikes. One church does things one way and another church does things another way.

This has resulted in all the different denominations, even though Christ only has one Church.

There was a time when I thought my theology was rather good. I had worked hard and studied hard. I had gone through all the usual theological subjects such as eschatology and I thought I had pretty good, solid theology. I was a Pastor and taught within my theological belief structure. But when I had an encounter with the Holy Spirit, the Lord showed me many things which went way beyond my theology. As good as I thought my theology was and as hard as I had studied to make it as solid as I possibly could, after an encounter with the Holy Spirit nearly all of my theology had to change. One of the reasons my encounter caused my theology to have to change was simply that my theology had put restrictions on God. My theology was too small and as such presented my God too small. My theology was constructed up until this point purely through intellect. But one of the things my encounter taught me was that our intellect alone makes our God too small. Our theology has to make way for God to be God. My theology had to expand and evolve to make way for what God was now revealing to me and sharing with me and showing me and even speaking to me with His audible voice.

When this encounter happened, I had a choice to make. Either, my theology would state, *"No God, you are wrong."* or, alternatively, *"WOW God! Now I need to expand my theology.*" My theology had to give way to the fullness of God so I could receive from Him. This is the reason why I believe the Bible doesn't tell us to have **unity in theology** but rather to have **unity in the Faith**. Here's the reason why it mattered. It is right that we have good theology, but more important that our theology is God given. When our theology is **God given** we have to remain in a position and in a place where we are saying,

> *"Holy Spirit, anytime you want to come and reveal to me and evolve and expand my theology then LORD, I'm open!"*

One of the most important things is that we are open. If we are not open, then God may come and reveal something to us but we use our theology as our plumb line and therefore conclude, *"No God, sorry, but my theology won't allow that."* That's making a huge mistake of dismissing revelation all because it doesn't fit into one's theological box, or theological arena. So we end up saying, *"Sorry God, I'm unable to agree with You there."* Then we have robbed ourselves. We have offended the Holy Ghost and robbed everyone else around us, especially if we are in a position within the five-fold ministry.

I tell my congregation that I may be teaching these things but they have their own Bibles and their own relationship with God. As long as they can hear His voice then they can go to God and ask Him themselves,

"God is this right, can you confirm this for me? I need to receive this for myself."

Do we allow our theology to determine the size of our God? Or do we allow our God to determine the size of our theology? Remember, you can`t walk in a revelation until you have received a revelation. You can hear a revelation but until you receive it, you cannot walk in it. When you receive it, you've got it. It becomes yours and part of your identity. That is you in Christ, the anointed one and His anointing. So we always have to be ready and available and say,

"God, I want to hear you."

By the way, nobody can hear God for you better than you. Jesus said,

"My sheep hear my voice." – John 10:27

We have to get into that position where we are still before Him, ready and expectant to hear Him. Let me encourage you to practise stillness. Stillness isn't doing nothing. Stillness is doing something. Being still is proactive. Being still, in this busy world, takes effort and discipline. So I want to encourage you to practise being still and knowing that He is God. It`s not about being still and sat there with your own theological restrictions, we are talking about being still and knowing that He is God and being open and willing and available to receive encounters and receive revelation. To be open to the Spirit of wisdom and revelation Ephesians 1:17 and for us to be ready to allow Him to expand and evolve our theology. My theology comes out of my relationship with Him. Whereas, my relationship with Him used to come out of my theology. I have learnt the art of expanding the tent pegs of my theology with great expectation.

There are times when our theology will need correcting. Sometimes I think I have understood something but, because of a revelation, I realise I was wrong in my theological standing in that area. Revelation blows you away. It blows your mind. You get so excited because you realise that it just came from heaven. Never allow yourself to be in a position where your theology creates a small God. That's the danger of small theology.

When we received faith, we received the ability for unity. A lot of people struggle to find unity, to find unity in their families and unity in their churches and yet God has given His people unity. We are carriers of unity. We have unity on the inside of us. The unity we have is found in the measure of His faith which He has given to us and dwells in us. Praise God we can have unity in the faith. The **commanded blessing of the Lord** comes to us when we have unity in the faith (Psalm 133). His faith is so holy and powerful, so precious and incredible, and purely supernatural. His faith is exactly that, it`s His and He has given us a measure of it. There's no unity in opinions and no unity in theology, no unity in so many of our churches as we have become ***theology centred*** rather than faith centred.

Unity in the faith is exactly that, it's in the faith (Ephesians 4:13). For us to have the commanded blessing of the Lord, we have to be walking in His faith. Only in His faith can we have unity. This is not something we have to work hard at as much as it's something we have to receive. I do not have any faith of my own. I only have what He has given to me. Only in His faith can I have and enjoy His unity.

I remember attending local Pastors' meetings and how every pastor there had their own theological background and their own ideas. Each knew they were different from the other and everybody was trying to find some common ground to make the meeting workable. I remember how, on one occasion, it was suggested we would take communion together and after some discussion it was agreed that this would be impossible due to the fact that one took communion with wafers and another with crackers and another with bread and so on. In the end it was decided that this just wasn't something we could do together. How sad is that? How far have we slipped from God's standards when we can't even come together and remember Him. Communion is about remembering what He has done and is doing and will continue to do. It's so we don't forget and we do this until He comes. Surely it shouldn't be about whether we use wafers or bread. I'm simply making the point here of how we fail to get unity in opinions. Our calling is to unity in the faith and this is very achievable.

In Acts 2 we read that the disciples were there in the upper room in one accord. When we think about this we realise that many of the disciples would have had different opinions and varying experiences and testimonies. There were times when some of the disciples were with Jesus and witnessed and were even directly involved in a miracle meanwhile some of the disciples weren't there with Jesus on that occasion. There were 120 men in the upper room plus women and children. So even there in the upper room it would have been impossible to have unity in anything other than the faith.

I believe that unity in the faith is something God's people need to get back to and something we need to realise afresh. Faith is God's. It is perfect It doesn't fail. Faith is never weak, it never takes a day off, it never has a break, it never retires. Faith is pure, holy, constant and reliable. To have His faith on the inside of us makes everything radical, incredible, everything precious and supernatural. The Bible says that faith without works is dead and so we need to activate this faith which He has put on the inside of us and we do that by stepping out as He tells us to.

Jesus said,

> "I only ever do what I see my Father in heaven do." — John 5:19

This should be our testimony too. If we were to take a boat out and step out to try to walk on the water, I'm pretty sure we would sink! Why? Because Jesus didn't say, "Come." And this is the whole point. We are only to do what we see our Father in heaven doing. Peter got out of the boat because Jesus said, "Come." And it was Peter's destiny to walk on the water. It was already written in heaven for Peter to walk on the water at this moment. I hope this begins to break you free from the confines of your theology. Our theology is way too small for our God. Or, to put it a better way, our God is too big for our theology.

When the commanded blessing of the Lord is in a local church, suddenly all the gossip and all the disharmony ceases. Each one of us should be busy being who He has called us to be and doing what He has called us to do. Jesus said that if a kingdom is divided amongst itself then how can it stand (Mark 3:24). So unity is of utmost importance.

These end times are waiting for the Saints to step up and to step out in unity and in faith and do great exploits; to do what Jesus did and the greater things still.

Chapter 3

The Sovereignty Of God

Matthew 16:13-17

"When Jesus came into the region of Caesarea Philippi, He asked His disciples, saying, 'Who do men say that I, the Son of Man, am?' 14 So they said, 'Some say John the Baptist, some Elijah, and others Jeremiah or one of the prophets.' 15 He said to them, 'But who do you say that I am?' 16 Simon Peter answered and said, 'You are the Christ, the Son of the Living God.' 17 Jesus answered and said to him, 'Blessed are you, Simon Bar-Jonah, for flesh and blood has not *revealed this to you, but My Father who is in heaven."*

Here's a really powerful revelation from this Scripture. Peter knew who Jesus was for one reason: Peter had received a revelation. Because of this revelation, Peter knew who Jesus was at a time when most people remained ignorant of His identity. When God gives you a revelation you might be the only one in a group of twelve, or a hundred, or a thousand, or the only person on earth who knows. But the bottom line is, when you get a revelation, you ***know***.

What we are looking at here is the truth that God is sovereign. It doesn't matter how good our theology is, we have to realise and be open to the truth that God can come in at anytime and change things. It's called the sovereignty of God. It doesn't matter how big we might believe God is, He can come and reveal the truth that He is a whole lot bigger than we first thought. We might think we have understood all there is to know about a subject but we have to acknowledge that God is sovereign and therefore can come at any time and place and reveal more. We need to learn even as we meet as the body of Christ that He can come and high-jack the meeting and turn our theology upside down. He can come and do whatever pleases Him. He is God and as such holds full rights to do so.

As demonstrated in the above Scripture, God can drop a revelation into a person so that suddenly they know something that they were ignorant of previously. Continuing along with this revelation, I'm now going to make a suggestion to you which will certainly get you thinking!

We see many times in Scripture that Jesus was impressed and even amazed by somebody's faith. Yet, we have learned so far in this book that nobody actually has any faith of their own. So how could Jesus meet people who had faith that impressed Him? Such instances as when Jesus said,

> *"I tell you the truth, I have not seen such great faith in all of Israel." – Matthew 8:9*

If man doesn't have any faith of His own and the only faith we have is the faith that God has given to us, then we can only conclude that every time Jesus met someone who displayed 'faith,' God must have already put that faith into them. Pause for a moment and consider that...that's huge. That's revelation!

God had literally put faith into certain people so that when Jesus walked this earth, He would meet the right people at the right time who had been already downloaded with His faith. Therefore, every miracle and healing was as a result of our God having gone before them and actually deposited a measure of His faith so as Jesus met these people with their different needs the ones which already had a deposit of faith would receive what they were predestined to receive. The crowds heard what Jesus said but these individuals were able to receive what Jesus said. The individuals who were pre-deposited with faith didn't just hear what Jesus said but they also responded. As we consider what I am suggesting here, don't lose sight of the truth that God is sovereign, He can actually do this just as He did to Peter in the opening Scripture of this chapter. Peter knew who Jesus really was because his Father in heaven ***revealed*** this to him. That was the only reason that he knew who Jesus was.

We can go deeper still here. Peter didn't even realise that he knew who Jesus was because he had received a revelation. It took Jesus to point it out to him. He didn't receive that in the natural, it wasn't a guess. It was a revelation from the Father in heaven. We learn here that God can just download us anytime He wants to. I don't want to get onto the subject of free will here but what I do want to say is that there are times when God will quite happily come and invade us. It's back to the sovereignty of God. He can step in anytime He wants and literally, with just one revelation, one encounter, He can change the very direction, the path of our entire life.

The Bible says that Jesus is the Alpha and Omega, the beginning and the end (Revelation 22:13). If you study that enough, you will conclude that He touched the end before He touched the beginning. Another Scripture declares that,

> *"...Before we were born He knew us."* – Jeremiah 1:5

When you start to ponder these things you may find yourself saying, *"This is too much. It's too big!"* Actually, that is meant to happen. Our minds are blown away inasmuch as they are transformed into the mind of Christ (Romans 12:2). Every encounter, every revelation and every faith experience that we live, means that our theology has to expand to make way for God. As the transformed mind evolves, our capacity to believe God is extended.

I'm basically suggesting here that God can and will be coming and invading us anytime He wants. I appreciate this is touching on the subject of free will, but just because God has given this to us doesn't mean that He, in His sovereignty, cannot overrule. God's sovereignty is bigger than our free will. He can come in at anytime and change things and thank God that He can and thank God that He does in His mercy and His love, His grace and His compassion for each and every one of us. The earth is the Lord's and everything in it (Psalm 24:1). God has not taken His hand from His creation and that includes us.

There are Scriptures for this:

Acts 9: Saul on the road to Damascus had a clear plan as declared in Scripture and that plan certainly didn't include him falling in love with Jesus and writing two thirds of the New Testament. Yet, as Saul journeyed along the road, 'suddenly' God shows up. Saul has an encounter of God and through that, the direction of his whole life changed forever. Instead of persecuting God's people, He becomes one of God's people. If God had not encountered him that day, Saul would have continued on his journey of destruction toward the early Church. Thank God that the sovereignty of God interjected with the free will of Saul.

Jonah decided to run away from God after he chose not to accept God's mission for him. The more Jonah ran, the more Jonah was confined, until we finally see Jonah in the constraints of the belly of a large fish with absolutely no way out. Jonah realises his attempts to not accept God's mission for him were exhausted and so repents, is vomited onto a beach, goes about completing his mission and shortly after is found sat down in a sulk (Jonah 4:5).

In Luke 4:28-30 we have an outraged group of people who decided to not only throw Jesus out of the synagogue and their city but were going to kill Jesus by throwing Him over a cliff. But, we see Jesus overruled their free will for their own good. Jesus had come to die for us and it was written exactly how that would happen and it certainly wasn't by a small and angry crowd throwing Jesus over any cliff.

> Verse 28: "So all those in the synagogue, when they heard these things, were filled with wrath, ²⁹ and rose up and thrust Him out of the city; and they led Him to the brow of the hill on which their city was built, that they might throw Him down over the cliff. ³⁰ Then passing through the midst of them, He went His way."

I'm sure with this revelation in mind you will come up with many Scriptures yourself as God reveals this truth to you. God in His sovereignty can, and does on occasion, overrule us.

I am now going to share with you what happens when God places His faith into an individual which causes that individual to act in a certain way.

Luke 8: The woman with the issue of blood who had suffered for over a decade, she had spent all of her money and seen just about every medical professional she could but still had her problem. Then she heard about Jesus and made up her mind that He could help her. This woman shouldn't have even been out among the crowd. Leviticus 15. Nonetheless, she went out, pushed her way through the crowd, touched the hem of Jesus' cloak and received her healing. Her faith, (***His faith in her***) caused her to receive her healing. His faith in this woman caused her to go where she shouldn't have been and to do what she should have not done; pushed through the crowd and reached out to touch Jesus' cloak. When His faith, in this woman, touched His cloak everything stopped! When Jesus stops ,everything stops. Jesus stopped and asked the question,

"Who touched me?"

The disciples pointed out that they were in a crowd and lots of people were brushing up against them. But Jesus was insistent, somebody had touched Him. He felt the virtue, the dunamis power leave Him. He felt something supernatural just happen. The woman stepped forward and explained the whole thing to Jesus and He declares that her faith had made her well.

Here is a massive lesson for us. When God's faith in us touches Him, that is when we receive our miracle. That's when we have an invasion of the supernatural right into the natural realm and into our circumstances. His faith, in us, is the only faith we have. When He gives us a measure of faith then that is enough to get the job done. Again, God had gone ahead and given certain individuals a measure of His faith so that when Jesus would meet these people during His ministry, something would happen which was preplanned and would be recorded in the Word of God forever. When His faith in us connects with His dunamus (Greek word for power) that's when we see supernatural results. When God gave this woman a measure of faith she was driven to connect with Jesus who was full of dunamus.

The Bible refers to our bodies as earthen vessels (2 Corinthians 4:7). Yet once we have given our lives to Jesus the earthen vessel becomes a temple filled with the Holy Ghost (1 Corinthians 3:16). The Bible is clear in Revelation 1:6 that we are priests and we are kings and Jesus is the great High Priest and the King of kings. So here am I, in my temple, as a priest and as a king. This is so exciting! We read in the Old Testament that the glory of the Lord so filled the temple that the priests couldn't function (2 Chronicles 5:14). That's the place that I want to be. Robert the priest, here in my temple, who cannot function because of the level of glory, the level of presence here in my temple. Just think about that for a moment. I once asked God,

"How much presence can any one man have and still function?"

Then He showed me!

Peter had so much anointing, his ***shadow*** healed the sick (Acts 5:15). Peter is a prime example of what I am saying here. Peter went out and his shadow happened to cover the sick people and they started crying out because they were getting healed and I'm sure Peter turned around to see what was happening and that was the first he knew about it. Peter the priest was busy living in his temple, which was so filled with the glory that Peter the priest wasn't functioning as much as the glory was functioning in Peter's temple. So as he was walking along, the glory and presence of the Lord healed the sick.

All praise to the God who knew us before we existed. All praise to the Alpha and Omega. All praise to the one who touched the end before He touched the beginning. All praise to the one who has already gone before us, who makes a way where there is no way. We are walking out a path that our God has already trod. A path onto which God is calling us; the supernatural path. The Bible says that we are in the world but we are not of it (John 17:16). It states that we are a peculiar people (1 Peter 2:9); that we are aliens (1 Peter 2:11). We are not meant to fit in to the world. We are just visitors here and we are not to act like the people of this world. We have to realise that we are priests who should be experiencing the overwhelming glory of God in our temples. Only then will we see signs, wonders, miracles and healing, resurrection and salvation like never before and we will reach a whole new level where we are actually doing the greater things that Jesus said we would do.

God has gone before us, God has put His faith in us. We see it right there in the Scriptures. As Jesus walked the earth He would connect with one person after another. Every time He connected, it was a divine appointment; it was destiny. Every time Jesus connected with somebody, into whom God had already poured a measure of His faith, Jesus would stop and a supernatural occurance would happen. We never have to get into a place of fear, worry nor concern. We are in the endtimes but God has already gone before us. He wrote the book and He is in complete control. He knows how it's all going to complete. Our responsibility is to go with the flow of the Holy Ghost. Remember, we carry His faith and His power and when the two touch there's always a glory explosion.

Chapter 4
How Faith Comes

How many times have we sat down and read some Scripture which went straight over our heads? A passage which was full of genealogies, for example, which leaves us feeling somewhat exhausted? Or we conclude, *"I don't get what that was all about!"* In this chapter we are going to look at the difference between reading the Bible as a book and reading the Bible and hearing God.

"So then faith comes by hearing and hearing by the Word of God." – Romans 10:17

So, if we want faith to come and we want faith to increase then it tells us here that Faith comes by hearing. The question we have to ask ourselves here is: When I sit down and read the Bible, am I hearing? Faith comes by hearing. So I get comfortable, open my Bible and begin reading it. Here's the possible issue, if I start reading but I don't hear God, then all I did was read it! We have to understand that the Bible is more than just a book. The Bible tells us that the Word became flesh and dwelt amongst us. In other words when we sit down and read the Bible we are not merely reading a book but literally we are sat down with Jesus. Now if we were to read the Bible like one would read any other book then it's quite possible that we can read it from cover to cover just like any other book and not hear God. I actually know of a guy right now who is 'searching' for God and has read the Bible from cover to cover and several other books from other religions and for him they were all just books. So again, it is possible to read the Bible as just a 'book.' If I read the Bible but I don't hear God, then all I did was read it, so faith didn't come!

Romans 10:17 — This verse says,

> *"So then faith comes by hearing and hearing by the Word of God."*

The Greek word for 'Word' used here is 'Rhema.' The Rhema Word is hearing God. There are two Greek words for Word. 'Logos' is the **written** word, the printed word, the Bible; 'Rhema' is the **spoken** Word, which is where we actually hear God. Faith comes by the Rhema Word. We learn and receive knowledge from the Logos word; something we have read in the Bible, historical facts, dates, information and stories. The 'Rhema' word means you can sit down and read a passage of Scripture you have read many times before but as you are sat reading you 'hear' God afresh. As you are reading the logos you suddenly hear God and so the logos becomes the Rhema. The logos Word was your foundation, you sat down with the already revealed Word of God. You were reading what is written on the pages. The Bible is printed in many different languages, many different versions and translations, but when we hear God we have moved from the logos Word to the Rhema Word. Remember, hearing God is what brings faith. Just reading what is in print is not necessarily hearing God to the extent which it brings faith. But, the Rhema Word is hearing God and that Rhema Word is what brings faith. Many of us have been there many times, we are reading a familiar passage of Scripture and suddenly we hear God speak to us and reveal something new from the familiar passage that we didn't previously know or see and this brings faith.

Our whole relationship with God is exactly that. It's a living, breathing relationship. It's intimacy, communion, fellowship, it's alive. Now, if our relationship with God is not alive then, what good is that? Who wants a relationship which is not alive; who wants a relationship which is dead? Marriages which go wrong, become sour as communication breaks down ,often go from bad to worse and frequently end up in divorce courts. It's of no use to anyone. In the same way God didn't give us a dead relationship with Him. God hasn't called us to *religion*, He has called us to a *relationship* with Him.

> "So then faith comes by hearing and hearing by the Word of God." – Romans 10:17

The **Rhema** Word of God. Faith comes when I hear God. We can hear God all of the time. I don't just hear God when I have my Bible open. I hear God non-stop whatever I might be doing. The Bible, 'logos', tells us this in the book of Revelation.

> "The Spirit is speaking to the churches, let him who has an ear hear what the Spirit is saying."

I hear God when I'm driving my car, sat on an aeroplane or watching the TV. Jesus said,

> "My sheep hear my voice."

He didn't say this was restricted to one's devotional time. Actually my whole existence is my devotional time, even when I'm doing something else. That is why the Bible says things like, 'pray without ceasing.' 1 Thessalonians 5:16. Relationship is a lifestyle but some people have been conned into thinking it's some kind of religious practice. That's when it becomes hard work, legalistic and boring.

We can all hear God in many different ways. We can hear God from within our ***imaginations***. God has been known to speak to people ***through animals***. (The Biblical account of God using a donkey to speak to Balaam who was riding it in Numbers 22.) There are open and closed ***visions, trances, night visions*** and ***dreams***. God sometimes brings other people to speak directly into our lives. We also may hear the ***audible voice*** of the Lord. God has a huge expectation that we will hear Him and has not placed limits on how. We are to be led of the Spirit and not led of the flesh so again we need to be able to hear Him. So when we hear God in the many different ways in which we can hear Him, then that is the 'Rhema' Word and not the 'Logos' Word.

I like to think of the Rhema Word as an extension of the Logos Word. If you hear a Rhema Word and then you go to the Logos Word and you cannot find anything there to back up what you have heard then you have to start to question, *"What did I hear?"* Maybe that wasn't God then! Every time you get a Rhema Word it should take you to the Logos Word for confirmation. This happens to me all the time. God will reveal something to me and I will be left weighing it up. I thinking to myself I didn't know that, I don't recall reading anything about that in the Bible. Then He will take me to the Logos and sure enough there it is. How did I never see that before?

Many times God will tell me to do something and I'm in awe having obeyed Him and then seeing the good 'fruit' from it. He will then begin to drop the relevant Scriptures into me regarding what He has done. It's so exciting when you have a living relationship with Him, when you are living it, breathing it, enjoying it. You will find yourself growing in Him at an incredible rate in your walk with God because this is what it is meant to be, a two way communication, a two way relationship. We love God because He first loved us. God has made this whole Christian life to be absolutely exciting. Even when difficulties come and challenges arise it's still to be exciting. Paul and Silas were falsely accused and arrested, flogged and finally imprisoned. In that prison cell, they began to pray and sing, to praise and worship, and the whole place shook under a heavenly visitation and the supernatural invaded their situation. It not only delivered them, but saw the jailor and his household saved and baptised that very night (Acts 16:25-34). We are called to run the race -not to stroll along it (1 Corinthians 9:24). Get yourself spiritually fit, get into training and 'run your race.' Run for Jesus. Run with everything He has given you. Get excited about God. This is not a small thing. This whole subject of faith is not a small thing. This is huge. This is supernatural and this is our God!

How does faith come? How does faith grow? How does faith increase? It's not by reading a book! You can read the Bible in the same way you can read any religious book and does faith come? No. Why not? Because you read it, you didn't **hear** it. To **read** the Bible is one thing; to **hear** the Bible is something else. When we spiritually hear the Bible, faith comes. When we read the Bible, but don't hear it, then it is read within the restraints of the individual's intellectual capacity. When we **hear** the Bible wth our spiritual ears it goes way beyond our intellectual capacity. It's when we hear the revelation and receive the revelation, it's when we hear the wisdom and receive the wisdom, that's when faith comes. Faith comes by hearing, ***so we need to be hearing***. The Spirit is speaking to the churches right now. Can we hear Him?

One of my favourite things is to invest time in people and help them to get started in their relationship with God and a massive part of that relationship is being able to hear God. Make up your mind today to hear God. Begin to expect to have visions and dreams. God speaks in so many different ways and just when you think you have listed all the possible ways in which God speaks to His people, suddenly we realise there are many more ways that we haven't yet considered. That's the sovereignty of God. We have to realise that God's ways are bigger than us. Yet in all the unmeasurable awesomeness of God still He came to bring us back to Himself (John 3:16).

The Father sent Jesus to come and rescue you and me. Once you receive wisdom and revelation and are led of the Holy Ghost you only then begin to realise just how massive all of this is. One of the things God has been doing with me lately, is that He gives me little glimpses into how big He is. Just the tiniest glimpse of how big He is leaves me undone in those moments and there are no words to describe those glimpses. God keeps revealing a little bit more, followed by a little bit more of who He is. He is so huge even a small glimpse is often more than I can sometimes handle.

It is difficult to put into words and difficult to relay to others, even just a glimpse of who He is and a glimpse of something of His size. A glimpse of His presence is just about impossible to try to convey to others. I know that part of the reason for this is because those glimpses are not merely seen with ones sight but are seen with ones whole being. The point of me even trying to bring this book to you is to endeavour to reveal something of our God and something of His Kingdom to encourage and spur us all on. The church is tiny compared with the Kingdom of God. The church is a tiny, tiny piece in a massive eternal Kingdom. Yet God ordained the church and He knows each one of us by name. As big as God is, He knows us each and every one.

The Bible tells us that the revealed things belong to us and to our children forever and that the hidden things belong to God (Deuteronomy 29:29). Yet I have learned that He wants us to tap into those hidden things too. It's His will that we do so:

> *"Call to Me and I will answer you and show you great and unsearchable things which you do not know." – Jeremiah 33:3*

We have to ask ourselves, *'What are we doing with the revealed things?'* Perhaps if we were doing something with the revealed things then we would be ready to receive some revelation of the hidden things. God so wants to share who He is with us. We are created in His image. I don't believe that He is wanting to hold back from us at all. We need to start calling on God. God instructed us through the prophet Jeremiah,

> *"Call to me and I will answer you…"*.

Let's immediately start to call to Him,

> *"Holy Spirit, are you there?"*

The revelations come out of the relationship. Call to Him. Do it now! He is more willing to answer us than we are to call.

It's in the calling that the revealing comes:

> *"Call to Me and I will answer you and show you great and unsearchable things which you do not know."*

Here is the key to the hidden things of God. Call to Him. It all stems from a living relationship with Him. God is more eager and excited to share the hidden things with His people than we are to receive them or to even bother going after them.

When you receive revelation like this, when you can hear God, when you receive that Rhema Word your faith increases even to the point that you are asking, 'What am I going to do with all of this?' And that's the key. You have to do something with all of this. The whole point of faith is that you do something with it. He gives us a measure of His faith so that we can please Him. Remember, faith without works is dead! You might have faith but what good is it if it is dead? Let's not carry around dead faith, but rather, living breathing active faith. Every time I hear God it increases my faith. That measure of faith He gave me when I gave my life to Him is increased every time I hear God. Every single time He invades me my faith levels rise, they increase and go through the roof. Hallelujah. Now let me ask you, who's believing God? Who's in a living relationship with God? And who's ready to go deeper?

I'm very fussy about the company I keep. The Bible warns us about this. Iron sharpens iron. I'm always on the lookout for iron. I want to hang out with iron. Hang out with those who are on fire, those who are also passionate, those who are running the race, those who are lovers of Jesus. Good faith company, keeps us in a good faith place. Encourage one another (1 Thessalonians 5:11).

Chapter 5

Faith Made Manifest

As we operate in His faith, *His* faith seemingly 'turns up'. In other words, it manifests and becomes visible through the miracles, healing and breakthrough. It suddenly happens and we see the faith in action right in front of us. Faith is the substance of things hoped for, the evidence of things not seen. It goes on to say that by it the elders obtained a good testimony (Hebrews 11). So we see the elders here through faith that obtained a good testimony. Faith will do that. Faith will give you testimony after testimony after testimony. It's what faith does. As soon as you pull the supernatural realm into the natural realm, which we do through His faith in us, we attain another testimony. This is how it works. Didn't even Jesus tell Peter off for his little faith...?!

I ask people to share a testimony with me and they go back maybe thirty or forty years or maybe longer and they share about the time when they gave their lives to Jesus. Now that's a great testimony to have and I hope we all have one like that. However, we are meant to have ***on-going*** testimonies not just that one of when we gave our lives to Jesus. We should have testimony after testimony, day after day, year in and year out. The longer we live the more testimonies we should have. Often, this is not what we see happening and the reason seems to be that many are not moving in this faith because they haven't had the faith revelation. The faith revelation is that the only faith we have is His faith and ***His faith works***. His faith is perfect. His faith never goes wrong. It's never weak and it never takes a break. His faith is constantly there and totally reliable, it's heaven sent and it's Gods. So testimonies should be a regular everyday occurrence for us. You and I should constantly be adding to our testimonies. It speaks in Revelation 12:11 about the blood of the Lamb and the word of our testimony…oh it's such a powerful combination! The blood of the Lord Jesus Christ together with the testimonies of the saints. The elders obtained a good testimony time and time again. How did they do that? They achieved this by operating in faith. Now who else wants a good testimony? I love testimonies and I want to get as many testimonies as possible.

Hebrews chapter 11 is about faith, faith, faith!

Lets look at some of the things that they were able to achieve as they were walking in His faith. Hebrews 11 verse 5:

"By faith Enoch was taken away so that he did not see death."

WOW! How impressive is that? By *faith* this happened to him. It goes on to say that he was not found because God had taken him. What's all that about? Look what faith did to Enoch. The Scripture goes on to explain how, before Enoch was taken, he had this testimony: he pleased God. How did Enoch pleased God? What had Enoch done? The Bible gives us the answer right at the beginning of verse 5, ***"By Faith…"***. The Bible says that without faith it is impossible to please God. The testimony of Enoch was that he pleased God. The Scripture here is underlining for us that faith was a massive part of his existence, faith was so huge in his walk with God that he was able to please God. May we all be able to have such a testimony, that we please God. If we want to please God then we have to have faith, and live faith. God's faith in us and flowing out from us. Therefore, we know here that Enoch pleased God. And because he pleased God, Enoch was taken away so that he did not see death and was not found because God had taken him. As we are walking in His faith, God will take us places that will blow our minds. God will place us in situations which are purely supernatural appointments and encounters. Faith opens up everything, the whole spiritual realm becomes open to us and available to us and we get to walk in it, run in it, soak in it. Look at how much we need His faith!

God both planned and purposed to give us His faith. I don't know how much this revelation is exciting you and spurring you on but I'm excited just sharing this. Think about this, that God has given us a measure of His faith. Hebrews 11 verse 3:

> *"By faith we understand that the worlds were framed by the word of God, so that the things which were seen were not made of things which are visible."*

This verse is declaring that God framed the worlds. In other words, as He spoke the words, *"Let there be..."* the Holy Ghost moved and created. So God has all the faith; we have a measure of that same faith.

We are pondering how powerful the faith of God is and considering what it actually means to be given a measure of His faith. The Bible speaks about calling things that are not as though they are (Romans 4:17). We have a measure of His faith. The Bible talks about the power of the tongue in James Chapter 5 and how the tongue is a small part of the body and yet the tongue has great power and this Scripture likeness it to a rudder on a ship, it's so powerful that it sets the direction of the ship and our tongues do the same. It sets the course of our whole body, our whole existence. So we have to learn to call those things which are not as though they are. So even when it looks like we are not blessed we start to confess that we are blessed. Why? Because we are doing exactly what scripture is declaring. So we call those things which are not as though they are, so we see our circumstances change for the better. We can see our lives move from the first part of John 10:10 to the second part of that verse:

> "The thief does not come except to steal, and to kill, and to destroy. I have come that they may have life, and that they may have it more abundantly."

If all we do is speak about how the devil is trying to steal, kill and destroy us then that's the very stuff we will watch him do. We need to start to call those things which are not as though they are. Declare you are blessed and the blessings come. All of this is to do with His faith. For too many of us His faith is sat there on the inside and, instead of living in this faith realm, we are living in lack and the first part of John 10:10. If we want to obtain a good testimony, even for ourselves, then we need to begin to call those things which are not as though they are. So, let the blind say they can see, the lame say they can walk, the sick say they are healed and so on; calling those things which are not as though they are. In doing so, we are calling God's faith in us to pull down – manifest – the signs and wonders, miracles, healing and breakthroughs right into our circumstances. Once we get this revelation we will realise that everything is subject to change because of God's faith in us.

Hebrews 11:6 says,

> "Without faith it is impossible to please God, for he who comes to God must believe that He is and that He is a rewarded of those who diligently seek Him."

Are we on fire for God, are we running after God, are we passionately pursuing Him? He is a rewarder of those who do this, who diligently seek Him. Verse 7 continues,

> "By faith Noah being divinely warned of things not yet seen moved with godly fear, prepared an ark for the saving of his household by which he condemned the world and became heir of the righteousness which is according to faith."

God tells him that He is going to flood the earth so needs him to build this really big ark. He gives Noah the dimensions and he sets to work. Noah didn't just hear the word but he also received it. When he heard the word he had to decide on his response. Noah therefore didn't just hear the revelation but he also received it and walked it out. He did something that he would never have been able to do if it wasn't for the faith God had placed in him. God's faith in Noah allowed him to do what no other man on the earth at the time was able to do.

Hebrews 11:8:

"By faith Abraham obeyed when he was called to go out to the place which he would receive as an inheritance and he went out not knowing where he was going."

If you and I are going to walk in faith then that's how it works. We are not necessarily going to know where we are going, but when God says, 'go', we go! We can only go when we have a measure of His faith in us. God's people who are flowing with Him are happy to go when He says to go. When we are flowing with God we don't need to know absolutely everything before we obey. All we need to know is His voice. Look how all of these people were blessed because of what they did. Noah was blessed because he ran with faith. Running with faith is running with God. Abraham got up and didn't even know where he was going and how blessed was he!

Verse 11: "By faith Sarah herself also received strength to conceive seed, and she bore a child when she was past the age, because she judged Him faithful who had promised."

God's faith in Sarah caused her to believe Him beyond her circumstances.

Let's just finish looking at some of the other names of faith people in Hebrews 11, like Moses...

Verses 24-25: "By faith Moses, when he became of age, refused to be called the son of Pharaoh's daughter, choosing rather to suffer affliction with the people of God than to enjoy the passing pleasures of sin..."

As a result of faith, Moses went in a different direction. He went in God's direction. Just look at all that Moses accomplished.

Verse 30: "By faith the walls of Jericho fell down after they were encircled for seven days."

What we are seeing here is faith in action and faith in action is testimony.

Verse 31: "By faith the harlot Rahab did not perish with those who did not believe, when she had received the spies with peace."

God had gone before her and given her the necessary faith so that when the spies came she responded accordingly. God will do that. God is sovereign. He will do what He wants, when He wants and how He wants. Never limit Him.

Verse 35: "Women received their dead raised to life again."

That's the level of faith they had. The dead raised to life again! Who is ready for the resurrections? We cannot see resurrections until we see faith. The only way we see faith is to step out in it and use it.

Verse 35: "Others were tortured, not accepting deliverance, that they might obtain a better resurrection. 36 Still others had trial of mockings and scourgings, yes, and of chains and imprisonment."

His faith in us is enough to get us supernaturally through anything.

Verses 37-38: "They were stoned, they were sawn in two, were tempted, were slain with the sword. They wandered about in sheepskins and goatskins, be-

> *ing destitute, afflicted, tormented – of whom the world was not worthy."*

The world is not worthy of 'faith saints.'

> **Verses 38-39:** *"...They wandered in deserts and mountains, in dens and caves of the earth. And all these, having obtained a good testimony through faith..."*

How do you get a good testimony? Through faith! If you are going to get a good testimony you have to get faith flowing. We have to start walking in His faith. It's the only way to get a good testimony.

Are we ready to receive a good report?

Hebrews 11:1-2:

> *"Now faith is the substance of things hoped for, the evidence of things not seen. For by it the elders obtained a good report."*

Now it is our turn.

Chapter 6

THE GIFT OF FAITH

We haven't even considered the subject of 'more than a measure.' There are people walking the earth right now who have more than a measure of His faith. That's right, there is such a thing as more. Didn't even Jesus tell Peter off for his little faith...?!

1 Corinthians 12:1-11 Spiritual Gifts

Unity in Diversity

Now concerning spiritual ***gifts***, brethren, I do not want you to be ignorant: You know that you were Gentiles, carried away to these dumb idols, however you were led. Therefore I make known to you that no one speaking by the Spirit of God calls Jesus accursed, and no one can say that Jesus is Lord except by the Holy Spirit.

There are diversities of gifts, but the same Spirit. There are differences of ministries, but the same Lord. And there are diversities of activities, but it is the same God who works all in all. But the manifestation of the Spirit is given to each one for the profit *of all*: for to one is given the word of wisdom through the Spirit, to another the word of knowledge through the same Spirit, to another faith by the same Spirit, to another gifts of healings by the same Spirit, to another the working of miracles, to another prophecy, to another discerning of spirits, to another ***different*** kinds of tongues, to another the interpretation of tongues. But one and the same Spirit works all these things, distributing to each one individually as He wills.

As we can see from the above Scripture, there is such a thing as a 'gift of faith' by the Holy Spirit (Verse 9). This is in addition to the measure of faith found in Romans 12:3. The measure of faith is what every one of God's people receives upon conversion. The gift of faith is something extra. This gift of faith is more than the measure! We know Peter walked on the water with a little faith so the extent of what is possible in the ***gift of faith*** is mind blowing. What are the limits of the gift of faith? God only knows.

Please don't use this as a reason not to move in faith. Remember faith the size of a mustard seed moves mountains and every one of God's people has a measure of faith, so we are all able to move mountains! Do you want the gift of faith? Are you presently walking in the measure? (2 Corinthians 5:7). I think once we are walking in the measure of faith, that is the time to consider the *gift* of faith. God decides who receives the individual gifts (Verse 11). But we can ask for the gifts! 1 Corinthians 14:1,

"Pursue love, and desire spiritual gifts..."

This verse is telling us that we can be in pursuit of spiritual gifts. If you want a gift, then ask Him.

Through the encounter that night with this whole revelation on faith, I have learned so much. But I think the biggest lesson for me has been the most exciting lesson and that's about walking by faith. We can have all the head knowledge there is to know, but if we are not walking in *faith* then we will fail at every turn. At this point in my journey I could literally write a book entitled '**Walking by Faith**'. That book would be full of testimony after testimony because that is what happens when we walk in His faith – good fruit in abundance. The blood of the Lamb, alongside testimonies, lead to yet more testimonies. The Kingdom of God never stops flowing and neither are we to stop flowing with Him.

Every time I preach, counsel somebody or pray for the sick, I am walking by faith. Whenever I move in a demonstration of the Spirit I'm walking by faith. Every time I prophesy or walk in any area of the kingdom of

God, I am walking by faith. Out of all the fruit in my ministry so far, not one has come without me walking in His faith. Now that's deep and worth pondering. The difference between knowing about God's Kingdom and flowing in His Kingdom is ***activated faith***.

As a full time Pastor of several decades, I sometimes find myself looking back and pondering some of the things I have done in faith. From some of the seemingly easier faith steps to the seemingly bigger stuff. I'm not sure whether one is actually bigger than the other as we are either walking in faith or we are not, but certainly through our human eyes we can evaluate, and compare one experience to another. For example, some years ago, a rather nervous lady came up to me in a meeting and was clearly distressed. She began to share with me what was going on in her life and she was afraid. As she was sharing with me I went into an open vision and I watched as the Lion of Judah stood watch over her and was roaring and roaring and roaring. I knew from what I was seeing that God had her situation under control and that all was going to turn out fine for her and her family. I was able to share the vision with her and she immediately began to relax as she understood God was showing her that things were not going to go in the direction she feared but that He was changing those circumstances for her. Well that all sounds rather good but she still left the meeting that evening the same way she came in albeit a little calmer knowing the vision I had over her. Now it was a matter of time. Several days went by, then months and finally the issue was resolved and everything was good. Thank You Jesus. So there is one example of faith in action, simply being there for somebody, hearing them out which is all walking by faith and then receiving and sharing a vision which in time proved to be right. So I would say that was an easy faith step for me in the part that I played.

Let's now look at what I would describe as some bigger faith steps, which I suggest took a whole lot more faith on my part.

One day I felt the Lord telling me to teach my congregation 'God defence'. This was at a time when many Christians and whole churches were coming under attack by so called 'radical extremists'. Congregations in different parts of the world were considering their security and some taking guns to church in case of any such attack. Not all countries allow guns and other such self defence weapons. I was about to leave my congregation for several weeks to travel and felt I was to teach them God defence. So I made the announcement,

> *"Today I am going to tell you about God defence and then immediately afterwards in a practical session demonstrate how to use it."*

Then came time for the demonstration, I picked up my iPad and selected a man right at the back of the church and instructed him that any time he was ready, to approach me and try to 'steal' my iPad out of my hands. He agreed, so I turned my back to him and the rest of the congregation and began to walk in the opposite direction. Some moments later, he came out of nowhere and I found myself in the middle of an attempted mugging. I immediately demonstrated the power of God defence and he was suddenly disabled and lay on the floor.

Here's my point, when I gave the man instructions to aid me in this demonstration, I really didn't have any idea how this would all go down. Was I going to end up looking really stupid and losing respect with all those people in my congregation? Was God really going to somehow intervene and defend me? The man 'attacking' me was after all a fellow Christian, this was more of a role play demonstration than a potentially dangerous mugging, hopefully nobody was going to get hurt, so was God really going to bother coming to my rescue when I didn't really need rescuing? These are the moments in my ministry which I sometimes find myself pondering,

> "Robert, why did you do that? You could have looked really, really stupid had God not have shown up. What if you had the whole thing wrong and He hadn't meant for you to demonstrate such a thing."

These moments of **what if** come flooding in and I realise, Robert, you took a big risk taking such a step and then I smile and know, but God moved, didn't He?! Hallelujah! Do you understand what I was referring to as some of the seemingly easier faith steps to some of the seemingly bigger stuff? The gift of faith is the Holy Spirit working through the believer empowering the individual to trust that God will act in a supernatural way at that time. I didn't stop there with the demonstration either, once I saw what God did to that man, I had the congregation experience this for themselves. I simply stepped to one side and gave instructions for the next scenario. I had someone attempt to steal a handbag belonging to a lady in a wheelchair. It was amazing what happened to them as the lady in the wheelchair called on Jesus. After several different scenarios were demonstrated that morning I then went on to interview the perpetrators and their testimonies were absolutely incredible of how God had disarmed them and taken them to the ground. Who said church was boring?

I have more recently been experiencing some incredible healings in the meetings. When I call somebody forward who is in pain and with every eye watching from the congregation, I speak to the individual and then respond as the Lord leads me, (the gift of faith operates alongside other gifts of the Spirit.) I will ask the question in front of the entire congregation, *"What's happened?"* I'm literally at that point stood out on the ocean of faith, waiting along with every other person in the meeting to hear the pending report. Praise God the testimonies are amazing and the healings are so many.

It's these moments I see as seemingly bigger faith steps than me giving a prophetic word, even a prophetic word over a nation. I guess because they take you right outside of any comfort zone and find you in a place of pending public failure if you've got it wrong. However, when we see God move in these moments we realise the joy and blessings of ***walking in faith***.

Although it's all His faith, whether the ***measure*** of faith or the ***gift*** of faith, it's the ***gift of faith*** that takes us far out of our comfort zones. It is much later that you might find yourself pondering the, 'what ifs' of the situation. At least that's my experience and testimony anyhow. If we want to see what faith can do we have to be prepared to move in it and to allow faith to move us.

We see in the Bible that the gift of faith is accompanied by great works of faith.

Acts 3:1-10:

> "Now Peter and John went up together to the temple at the hour of prayer, the ninth hour. And a certain man lame from his mother's womb was carried, whom they laid daily at the gate of the temple which is called Beautiful, to ask alms from those who entered the temple; who, seeing Peter and John about to go into the temple, asked for

alms. And fixing his eyes on him, with John, Peter said, 'Look at us.' So he gave them his attention, expecting to receive something from them. Then Peter said, 'Silver and gold I do not have, but what I do have I give you: In the name of Jesus Christ of Nazareth, rise up and walk.' And he took him by the right hand and lifted <u>him</u> up, and immediately his feet and ankle bones received strength. So he, leaping up, stood and walked and entered the temple with them – walking, leaping, and praising God. And all the people saw him walking and praising God. Then they knew that it was he who sat begging alms at the Beautiful Gate of the temple; and they were filled with wonder and amazement at what had happened to him."

In this Scripture we see the gift of faith in action. As seemingly nothing happened when Peter prayed. The lame man is still sat there lame. Then in Verse 7 Peter took the lame man by the right hand and lifted him up and it was at that point that the healing manifested. This extra step, this gift of faith in operation, is exactly what we are talking about in this chapter.

Many of us would shy away from pulling the lame man to his feet and would have stopped after the prayer and concluded, the man wasn't going to be healed. We then often find ourselves not praying for people again as we are doubting and considering the, 'what if nothing happens' scenario. We must remember that faith is God given and that we don't have any faith of our own; that His faith works and that there's nothing wrong with a little faith. That's how Peter walked on water and that same little faith can move mountains.

This is your time to start walking by faith…to see what His faith in you will accomplish.

www.ingramcontent.com/pod-product-compliance
Lightning Source LLC
Chambersburg PA
CBHW051706090426
42736CB00013B/2563